THE PERFECT SWING FUNDAMENTALS

by Fred Haney

Jeff,

Enjoy the journey of golf.

Fred Haney

The Perfect Swing Fundamentals
© Copyright 2010 by Fred Haney
All rights reserved
Printed in the United States of America

No part of this publication may be reproduced without
the written permission of the author.

Cover design, illustrations and layout by Ed Carson
Photography by Tom Treick

TABLE OF CONTENTS

ACKNOWLEDGEMENTS

I am forever grateful to my mother and father for introducing me to golf at the age of 10 and then supporting my love with such an amazing game throughout the rest of their lives.

Thanks also to my beautiful wife Reggie who has listened to me talk about writing this book for way too many years. Her unwavering support and love allowed me to complete this project.

A special thanks goes to my good friend Jim Damis. Jim was very persistent in encouraging me to write this book, and helped me greatly in organizing and editing. This book would never have been written without the many nudges, pushes and prods by Jim. We share the belief that this book will forever change the way golf is taught, and that is a very good thing for future golfers.

Tom Treick took the photos for this book and Ed Carson did an amazing job of digitally enhancing those pictures and putting everything together for publishing. Thank you for your help in making this book possible.

CHAPTER 1: THE PERFECT SWING CONCEPT

Stand at the end of any busy golf driving range and watch golfers of all abilities swing a golf club. Most of the swings you'll see are not very good--they don't produce consistently accurate shots nor do they produce much power. You may spy an occasional golfer who will produce decent enough shots with a swing that looks very complicated. More than likely you will spot a player or two with a pretty looking golf swing that either doesn't deliver much power or badly miss-hits the ball once in a while. There are as many different golf swings as there are muscles in the body.

Now stand at one end of the driving range tee at a Professional Tournament and notice the variety of swings. While most have a certain rhythm and they all seem to have enviable power, there are differences between swings that are easily detected by the naked eye. Players such as Jim Furyk on the PGA Tour and Jim Thorpe on the Senior Tour have very awkward looking, complicated swings yet are known as excellent ball strikers. Jack Nicklaus, Lee Trevino, and Tiger Woods have swings very different from each other. Yet they were three of the best players in the history of the game.

The reality is that there are many different ways to swing a golf club. Some are just a lot more complicated than others, and harder to teach or learn. Professionals such as Tiger Woods and Phil Mickelson, as great as they are, continue to make changes in their swings. I can guarantee you that they are not trying to make their swings more complicated or harder to repeat. Virtually every tour player's swing is in a constant state of flux--making a takeaway change, a posture change, a downswing change, a balance point change, you name it. The idea is to make their swings easier to do and more efficient. They may have shot 63 one day two weeks earlier, but now are committed to making a swing change. They know that under pressure only the simplest, most efficient swings will consistently hold up.

Announcers on TV golf broadcasts, most being either renowned former players or renowned golf instructors, are always pointing out small problems or deviations from the norm in even the best looking and most efficient swings. Most of the time the TV viewers are not given any explanation of what the ideal swing would be like, only the problem that caused the player's bad shot.

What are the world's best golfers trying to achieve? What high standards in the golf swing are the TV announcers alluding to? Is there possibly a perfect swing, or at least a perfect swing model with which to measure all swings? A swing that hits perfectly accurate and powerful shots every time. My answer is yes.

My definition of the "Perfect Swing Model" includes 4 general requirements. First, it must produce the most powerful and efficient swing possible. Golf courses are long. The shorter a golfers' average drive the more difficult the game becomes. Hitting a golf ball right down the middle every time, but only 100 yards per drive, is simply not acceptable for most golfers.

We have all seen golfers who hit the ball a long ways by using brute force rather than excellent technique. Very few make their way to the PGA tour and those that do have at least decent technical skills. The best swings on any professional tour always look relatively easy compared to how far the ball travels. When Tiger Woods hits a drive 340 yards it looks like he swings hard and fast, but when he hits a smooth 300 yard drive the effort does not seem nearly enough to generate such power. Certainly all golfers are limited by their size, strength and flexibility, but efficient technique can maximize power for almost everybody. As you will see, the main ingredient for efficient power is a body turn, so golfers with certain physical handicaps, or those severely overweight or elderly and unable to turn are not candidates for using a perfect swing. It has been my experience, however, that many golfers insist that they cannot turn enough to generate power when in fact they can. Learning where the turning action comes from and what blocks it from happening can help most golfers turn further and faster than they had ever imagined.

The second requirement for the Perfect Swing Model is that it returns the club head solidly to the golf ball. A swing that produces great club head speed is of no use if it doesn't strike the ball solidly. The "Principle of 45" is probably the most important yet least understood fundamental of a good golf swing and combined with the fundamental of swinging the club "on plane" insures that the ball will be solidly struck. Hard to do? Not at all. Most golfers' swings are much more complex and difficult to repeat than The Perfect Swing Model.

Requirement three is that the golf ball is hit straight at the target without any manipulation of the clubface with the arms and hands. At the speed a powerful swing travels, to try and hit a golf ball straight by rolling one arm and hand over the other makes no sense. A non-manipulative swing is simpler and under pressure will hold up much better. Simple is good. Difficult requires much more talent and hard work.

The fourth requirement is that The Perfect Swing must involve the least amount of active muscles. Those muscles not actively participating in the swinging of the club may be supporting the club or our body structure, or they may just be going along for the ride. It always gets back to being simple. And powerful. And accurate.

In following chapters I will lay out the fundamentals of the perfect swing. A couple of these fundamentals--The Principle of 45 and The Principle of squareness/sameness you may not have even heard of. Yet they are vital to making a perfect swing as well as understanding what you may do right or wrong in your own swing.

You will also find that a couple of long time accepted fundamentals of swinging a golf club aren't what they seem and quite probably are at the root of what ails your game. The knowledge you can glean from this book may be difficult for some to understand and difficult for others to accept. It can also lead to making the changes to create a more powerful, more accurate and simpler golf swing.

The Perfect Swing requires a perfect setup. Virtually every golf instruction book and most golf instructional magazines include articles on making a better grip, better body and club alignments and better posture. I am convinced that only an absolute beginner in the game would not have a good idea of how to set up to a golf ball. Rather than start with Chapters on the grip, posture and alignments and bore those who have read thousands of articles on them, I have placed those chapters near the end of the book. Since the perfect swing requires a perfect grip, posture and setup, they will be assumed throughout. If you have confusion regarding those elements, please feel free to start with those chapters.

CHAPTER 2: POWER

The game of golf is about hitting a small ball accurately and precisely while covering long distances in the fewest strokes. If the average golfer could gain 20% more length on his shots, his scores would come down considerably. Take 20% length off of Tiger Woods game and he would still be good, but he would struggle to make cuts on the PGA Tour instead of being the best player in the world. Creating controlled power is the very essence of golf. The golf clubs do not do the work themselves, as is so often suggested. The player needs to use his muscles to apply power to move his clubs.

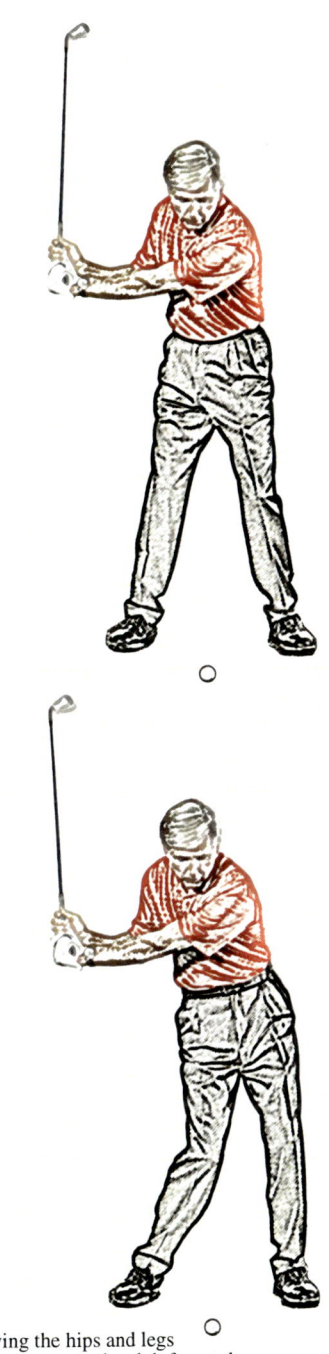

Where does that power come from? It comes from two places--the turn of the body and the loading and unloading (re-leasing) of the arms and hands. Let's take a look at these aspects of power separately.

Moving the body can move a golf club all over the place, but we want to move the club accurately and with efficient power. What parts of the body are useful and what parts are not? Lets start with the legs and hips. Turning the legs and hips, without actively moving any other muscles does not move the club back and forth. It just sits there. In other words there is absolutely no power at all generated from the hips, legs and feet. All the talk about Nicklaus

Moving the hips and legs does not power the club forward.

generating his power from his big legs and all the golf articles advising to push off the right leg to hit the ball farther were nothing more than baloney. The legs, feet and hips can restrict power as will be explained in the chapter on Swing Blockers, but it is impossible for them to add any power. In a perfect swing they will only support the body and hold balance. Basically they only go along for the ride. This is great, because the fewer active muscles involved in the swing the easier it is to do well.

How about turning from the shoulders, long accepted as the preferred way of swinging the club back and forth? Yes, that definitely will move the club and create the power that propels a golf ball a long way. There are two problems though. First, turning the shoulders by themselves does not turn the hips or move the legs. This naturally creates an over-the-top or outside-in swing path. Secondly, turning from the shoulders moves the shoulders-arms-hands triangle to the impact position before the middle of the body, resulting in an open clubface (slicing). Neither an off plane swing path nor an open clubface are acceptable for a perfect swing. Making compensations for those swing errors is complicated and unacceptable as well.

The perfect turning motion comes from the torso, below the shoulders but above the hips. The muscles in the front of the torso, the abdominals, are of no use because they pull the upper body forward as when doing a stomach crunch. The muscles in the back and at the sides, the lats and obliques are the key to power. The obliques are especially suited for swinging a golf club, because they will turn both the shoulders and the hips. The obliques wrap diagonally around the torso and actually crisscross with one layer of muscle over the top of another. Their job is to cause a rotational movement of the torso. Best yet, they time the turning motion perfectly. The obliques turn the hips half as far and half as fast as they turn the shoulders and allow the body to reach the finish of the release in the proper order--torso first, followed by the hips and shoulders.

The lats have a relatively minor role of lifting and holding the arms in the proper top of the backswing position. The slower the backswing and the longer the pause at the top of the swing the more the lats must be used for lifting and holding the arms due to lack of swing momentum.

The turning of the torso needs to be around our spine, because of the way we are built. Turning on the backswing around the spine, the center of mass of our torso moves from centered in the stance toward our right leg and foot. As we turn forward that mass moves past center to the left leg and foot. Perfectly done, the spine should stay in the same place until the finish of the release. The forward momentum of the torso turning helps thrust through the resistance of striking the ball and maximizes power. If we were to turn around the center of the torso the center of mass would stay centered and there would not be as much thrust through the resistance of hitting the golf ball. Imagine pushing a heavy object sideways. If your torso and your arms move together as you push, the object will move easier than if your torso remains stationary.

To give an example of what this means lets assume a golfer makes perfect contact with a golf ball with the club head traveling 100 miles per hour. The ball and club head stay in con-

The oblique muscles (shaded) have perfectly turned the torso.

tact with each other for approximately an inch. In a perfect swing around the spine the club head may lose only 10 miles an hour in that inch due to resistance from the ball and ground. In a swing where the turn is around the center of the torso the club head could lose as much as 20 miles per hour, resulting in much less ball speed and a much shorter shot.

Turning isn't the only source of power. At address the arms hang extended at each side of the torso. On the backswing the right arm should bend at the elbow approximately 90 degrees as the left arm comes across the chest. The wrists, uncocked at address, cock fully by the top of the backswing.

The bending of the right arm, the left arm moving across the chest and the wrists cocking are the components of the loading of the arms and hands. On the downswing the turning torso delivers the loaded arms and wrists to the release point. No effort should be made to swing the arms and hands forward with the arms and hands. A constant acceleration by the turning torso will keep the loaded arms and wrists loaded. Once the torso stops accelerating the loaded arms and wrists will automatically begin releasing. The release continues until both arms are straight and at each side of the torso and both wrists are fully uncocked. This crack-the-whip type of action adds tremendous speed to the club head. The automatic release applies to any swing length or speed. The only requirement is that the

The left arm, right arm and wrists are all loaded perfectly.

downswing turning motion be accelerated at a constant rate to the release point. That is achieved by feeling a constant pulling pressure in the armpit areas where the arms are connected to the turning torso.

The loading and unloading is not as complicated as it sounds. A perfect swing requires no manual use of the hands, wrists or arms to move or power the club. The turning torso moves the arms back and forth. The triceps provide structural support (more on this in Chapter 6). The biceps have no job at all.

Could the wrists and arms be used to power the club? Sure. However, your wrists will automatically uncock much faster than you can manually make them uncock. The same goes for your right arm releasing. Plus, manually straightening the right arm almost always leads to minor hyperextension of the right arm which in turn leads to tendonitis or golfers elbow. Adding to the problems is trying to manually time the release for different swing speeds and swing lengths in order to hit a variety of shots. Remember, even on a half speed swing the release happens in a split second. So manually releasing takes more muscular effort and produces less power and accuracy--in other words highly inefficient and inconsistent.

The simplicity of creating efficient power in a golf swing can be summed up by the following: Turn and load, turn and automatically release. This is similar to a baseball pitcher throwing a fastball except the golf swing biomechanics are simpler. The pitcher turns and loads his arm and wrist, then he turns and releases or throws. The baseball throwing motion requires actively using arm and wrist muscles to throw the ball fast. In a golf swing we hold on to a long lever, the golf club, which enables us to just allow the arms and wrists to load and release automatically for the most power and accuracy. In a Perfect Swing the wrists and arms offer support only--their load and release for power is actively created by the turn of the torso.

If it seems like I have left something out, you are right. What do we turn and release at? The answer for now is that we do not release at the golf ball. The release is the most misunderstood aspect of the golf swing by all levels of golfers (including instructors) and I will cover it very thoroughly in the Chapter on The Principle of 45. So for now we know how to create power, but not harness it. The next several chapters are all about increasing precision without increasing difficulty.

CHAPTER 3: SWING PLANE

In the previous chapter we learned how to develop power. Now we have to learn how to channel that power so that the club actually hits the ball. One major requirement is that we swing the club on plane with the golf ball.

Swinging the golf club on plane is one of the most important fundamentals for playing good golf. You can't pick up a golf magazine or instructional book that doesn't at least refer to being on or off plane. Many will have major articles about how to swing on plane. Yet very few golfers really understand what on plane really is and even fewer know if they are on or off plane during their own swings.

Some articles about swing plane have tried to define it. A common definition is that the club is on plane any time the lowest end of the club points to the target line and, when the club is parallel to the ground it is also parallel to the target line. While entirely correct, this definition draws a collective "huh" from at least 50% of all golfers. Another problem is that it includes a lot of on plane possibilities that require difficult manipulation by the arms and hands. Those manipulations can reduce accuracy and cause power leakage.

Let me give you a better way to define being on plane, one that meets the simple, efficient criteria of the perfect swing. The definition of being on the perfect swing plane is when the club is in position to return and strike the ball down the target line without any arm or hand manipulation. It really is that simple. Grab a club and try the following experiment.

Grip the club with the right hand only and set the club behind the ball. Now swing the club away from the ball with your right arm until the butt end of the club points to the ball. Let the club swing back to the ball naturally, with support by the arm and hand but no manipulation. As you see, the club strikes the ball. Why? Because the club was on a perfect plane that required no manipulation to hit the ball. Next, take the club back from the ball to where the butt end of the club points several inches inside the ball (toward your toes). Again let the club swing naturally with support by the arm and hand but no manipulation. The club will strike the ground several inches inside the ball. You can repeat this with the club pointed at a spot several inches outside the ball if you wish. The club will swing above the ball, not ever touching the ground.

So now we know that the club is perfectly on plane with the ball when it is in position to naturally swing back to the ball without any arm or hand manipulation. But how does that knowledge help us when we are swinging a club and not looking at where the butt end of the club is swinging. With a mirror, glass door or other reflective surface behind you do the above experiment again. When you have the butt end of the club pointed to the ball look at your reflection. Notice that the part of the clubshaft that is the same height as the right shoulder is in line with that shoulder. On the backswing, if the club travels toward the right shoulder it is always on the perfect swing plane. As the club head moves higher off the ground than the right shoulder the club is on the perfect swing plane if the part of the club or left arm that is the same height as the right shoulder is in line with the shoulder. This will always apply, no matter how tall or short you are, how wide your shoulders are, what length club you are using or unusual stance or setup is necessary. If the club always travels toward the right shoulder on the backswing the angle of the plane will be ever changing, but the club will always be on plane and require no manipulation to stay on plane.

We are getting closer to what we all want--a simple way to know if we are on a perfect swing plane. But there are never any mirrors behind us when we play golf. Thank goodness for that. So how do we know if our club is traveling toward our right shoulder? Put your grip on a club and look down at it. Notice the clubshaft is in line with a part of the top of the right hand and a part of the top of the left hand. We will talk more about the grip in a later chapter, but no matter how you grip the club, some part of each hand will be in line with the clubshaft. Now make a backswing and instead of focusing on where the club goes, focus on where the swing moves the hands. <mark>All we have to do to keep the club on the perfect plane is to allow that portion of the right and left hands that are in line with the clubshaft to travel toward the right shoulder. The part of the fingers on both hands that are in line with the bottom side of the shaft may be used as a guide as well.</mark>

Most golfers will find moving their hands toward their right shoulder on the backswing easy to feel and do. This is because it will naturally happen if your left arm stays in the same relationship with the left side of your torso and there is no hand or arm manipulation. If you have problems swinging the club toward your right shoulder, try moving your hands toward your right hip, your right ear or the top of your head just to feel the difference. For some there will be a confidence issue, trusting that their sense of feel is accurate. For those who have swung the club in a non perfect swing plane it will take a certain amount of practice

Clubshaft on plane with the ball and right shoulder on backswing.

swings to make a change. The more practice swings you make without a ball the faster the change will happen. Using a mirror or other reflective surface to watch your backswing can substantially reduce the time needed to make a swing plane change.

The perfect swing requires the golf club to remain on plane at all times. On the downswing the club head travels on the same arc away from the right shoulder toward the ball. As the club head passes the impact position it should always travel toward the left shoulder which means that the hands always travel toward that shoulder as well. Since the club is on plane at the top of the backswing and naturally is staying on plane on the forward swing the momentum of the club and the structure of our body helps keep the club on plane to the end of the follow through. There will be more on this in the chapter on The Principle of Squareness/ Sameness.

Other than the right shoulder on the backswing and the downswing, and the left shoulder on the follow through there is one other body part on plane with the club and ball during the perfect swing. During the release through impact the right forearm must be on plane with the clubshaft. When viewed down the target line from behind the

Clubshaft on plane with left shoulder on follow through.

golfer it appears the clubshaft is an extension of the right forearm at impact. With a perfect grip and setup, a perfect turning motion and proper support by the arms and hands the right forearm will automatically be on plane in the hitting area--manipulation by the arms and hands to guide the right forearm to an on plane position is not necessary.

Great golfers of the past have shown that you don't have to stay on what I have described as the perfect plane to hit fantastic shots. All great golfers are on plane in the hitting area, but many are not on plane during their backswings. A few violate the swing plane during the first part of the downswing, but not by very much. But they all have to make the necessary correction for their off plane idiosyncrasies if they wish to hit great shots. There are plenty of ways to hit those great shots, some are just a lot harder than others.

At this point we know how to produce power by making a perfect "turn and load and turn and release." We also know how to keep the club on plane so that power is directed toward the golf ball. But does that necessarily mean we will strike the ball solidly every time? Not yet. In the next chapter we will learn the fundamental that allows the delivery of the power solidly to the ball.

CHAPTER 4: THE RELEASE AND THE PRINCIPLE OF 45

As explained in the previous chapters the perfect swing requires the club to swing on a perfect swing plane. Power for that perfect swing is generated by turning the torso and the load and release of the arms and wrists. The forward turn of the torso delivers the loaded arms forward with speed and in position to be released. What happens next is probably the most misunderstood part of the golf swing.

To understand the release you must know what you are releasing at. Let's compare to a baseball pitcher. Like a golfer the baseball pitcher turns his body 90 degrees away from his target and loads his right arm (wrist cocked and arm bent 90 degrees at the elbow.) The pitcher then turns to the target and releases his right arm (straightens his arm and uncocks his wrist at the target) to throw a fastball. If he turns his chest perfectly toward his target and releases his arm and wrist perfectly toward the target the ball goes where it was intended. If the turn is not perfectly to the target, it is very difficult for the pitcher to manipulate his arm and throw the ball to the target. If the pitcher turns correctly but fails to release the arm and wrist perfectly toward the target then the fastball is definitely going to the wrong spot.

Does the same hold true for a golf swing? If we turn and release at the golf ball perfectly do we hit perfect golf shots? Most golfers answer "yes." The correct answer is no. Try addressing a golf ball with the ball centered in the stance. If you turn your torso so that your chest faces the ball at impact and your right arm straightens at the ball you will hit way behind the ball--approximately 45 degrees behind the ball. Beginning golfers are famous for trying to release right at the golf ball, with disastrous results. Either they hit bone jarring fat shots or they raise slightly and completely whiff the ball (the club swings upward as it passes the low point of the swing well behind the ball.) So what should we release at in the perfect swing?

The second most common answer to what should we release at is "the target," meaning where we want the ball to fly. That could still be considered similar to the baseball pitcher's release. But if you turn your torso to the end target and then straighten your right arm to that target the club head flies well above the ball without touching it. Again, the question of what do we release at remains unanswered.

If you are guessing by now that we must turn and release the loaded right arm to a spot on the ground between the ball and the end target you are correct. The question is--exactly where is that spot? Let's go back to the example of releasing exactly at the golf ball. The club strikes the ground approximately 45 degrees behind the ball. It makes sense then, to hit the ball solidly we must release to a spot 45 degrees ahead of the ball. And that is exactly where we need to turn and release for perfect contact with a ball positioned in the center of our stance.

Fully loaded arms and wrists at the release point.   Finish of release to 45 degrees ahead of center of stance.

I have called this very important fundamental the Principle of 45. If you look at the swings of all the great players on any of the worlds golf tours you will see that they all release to the same place. Both arms become straight at approximately 45 degrees ahead of the middle of their stance. At that point their arms are at their sides in the same relationship with their torso as at address. The golf club, which had been behind the chest before the release, is now directly in front of the chest. The release is a catching up of the arms, hands and club to the upper body of the golfer.

When the ball is positioned at the center of the stance the perfect release to the 45 will strike the ball first. The club will contact the ground under the front edge of the ball. This is an appropriate strike for all good players when using a wedge or short iron, or perhaps when hitting a lower flighted shot with a longer club. But if we move the ball forward in our stance to hit a normal shot with a 5 iron, 3 wood or driver do we still release to 45 degrees ahead of the center of our stance? The answer is yes.

As good players move from their short irons to more straight faced clubs they move the ball progressively more forward in their stance. I will cover this more thoroughly in the chapter on Perfect Alignments. Yet all the great players always release to the same place unless they are hitting an unusual specialty shot. If a player has the ball positioned 2 inches ahead of center in the stance and releases to 45 degrees ahead of center the club will strike the ball first and strike the ground under the center of the ball--perfect contact for a normal long iron or hybrid shot. If a player has the ball positioned 3 inches ahead of center in the stance the same release will strike the ball and the turf at the same time--perfect for the sweeping action of a fairway wood. With a driver played 5 to 7 inches ahead of center of the stance the club would strike the ground first if it were not teed up. Since it is indeed teed up, the club catches the ball properly at the bottom of the swing arc or slightly on the upswing. With all of these golf ball positions in the stance the release can be to the same point--45 degrees ahead of center in the stance. In other words, in the perfect swing the perfect release will work for all normal shots.

Only when the ball is played behind the center of the stance do we need to release to a different spot. Let's say you wanted to hit a very low shot and played the ball 2 inches behind center stance. If you released to 45 degrees ahead of center the leading edge of the club would strike the middle of the ball and contact the ground an inch ahead of the ball producing a somewhat bladed shot. ==To make the proper contact with the ball the release should be to 45 degrees ahead of the ball when it is played behind the center of the stance.==

The arms, hands and golf club don't catch up to the turning torso until the finish of the release at 45 degrees ahead of center stance. ==In other words, if you start with a square body alignment at address the shoulders and chest will be open to the target line at impact.== In fact, the shoulders and chest are almost completely turned to the finish position by impact with the ball.

Cocking the wrists while at address position.

The sequence of the release is another important but very misunderstood aspect of the golf swing. Many golfers think that the wrists are the last thing to release and they try to delay the release of the wrists on the downswing. This is an invitation to a shanked shot. Let me explain. In the address position and in the impact area the wristcock or uncock motion is off plane. That motion would move the club approximately 90 degrees off of the proper swing plane. Once the body has turned back far enough or the right arm has bent enough or a combination of the two motions, the hands will have traveled past the right hip. As the hands pass the hip in the perfect swing the wristcock motion becomes on plane. Therefore all wristcock or uncock needs to happen in the zone where the hands are between the right hip and the top of the backswing. If a golfer holds his wristcock too long on the downswing the cocked wrists and hands will pass the right hip. The uncocking motion will then throw the club head outside the correct plane with the usual result being a shank.

If you take a look at all of the great players of this game of golf they all look very similar at impact. Their wrists have uncocked completely by impact yet their right arms are still bent and their left arms are still slightly across the left front of their torsos. In the perfect release, the body stops accelerating which allows the wrists to start uncocking, the right arm to start straightening and the left arm to start moving back across the chest. Yet by impact, only the wrists have completed their release. The right and left arm are not completely released until 45 degrees past the center of the stance.

If the perfect release seems difficult, it isn't. To manually create and time the release with your arms and hands could be incredibly difficult, but the perfect swing only requires that our body turn accelerate to a certain spot and let the automatic release

The wrists are fully released at impact, but the right arm is still being straightened.

catch the hands and arms up to the body. The way to learn where the body turn acceleration stops and the release starts is actually to monitor where the finish of the release occurs. If both arms become straight at 45 degrees past the center of the stance you've got it. If the release ends short of 45 degrees past center stance your body turn needs to accelerate a bit further until the finish of the release is perfect. If your release ends beyond 45 degrees past the center of your stance, well, you have become a very accomplished player and can easily adjust your release.

Constant acceleration of the body turn feels smooth. If a player starts the downswing too fast he may not be capable of keeping the constant acceleration long enough to release to the perfect spot. The best spot to monitor the feeling of a smooth , accelerating body turn is where the arms connect to the body. As the downswing starts you will be able to feel a certain amount of pressure in both armpit areas. It should never feel jerky. When the pressure eases the release is finished. With practice it will become a trustworthy feel for all swings.

When the turning torso stops accelerating does it come to a complete stop in the downswing? No, it just stops going faster. The torso doesn't stop turning until well into the follow through. As in the child's game of crack-the-whip, the turning center will slow down almost to a stop at the 45, but the momentum of the club catching up to the turning torso carries the torso farther around.

The knowledge of what to actually release at can be very empowering. No mystery, no doubt as to whether you can hit a shot solidly. Less fear when needing to carry a water hazard or greenside bunker. So does everything we have learned so far about the perfect swing guarantee we hit the ball straight as well as solid and far. Probably, but there is one more extremely important piece of information golfers should know. I call it the Principle of Squareness/Sameness.

CHAPTER 5: THE PRINCIPLE OF SQUARENESS/SAMENESS

Knowing how to hit a golf ball solid and far is not enough to become a good player. Golf courses have plenty of obstacles and hazards which need to be avoided. We need to know how to hit a golf ball straight.

In the past, golf instruction has focused on trying to be square at impact, which would seem logical if it weren't so doggone difficult to do. Some of the most respected teachers of the game have repeated an old myth about Ben Hogan keeping his clubface square to the target longer than any other player--as much as 17" in the impact area. Apparently, they must have flunked geometry and physics classes.

Let's look at some facts. First, the club head can be traveling more than 100 miles per hour in the impact zone. Though the clubface starts square to the target at address it faces 90 degrees open at the top of the backswing as well as halfway back down. When the release starts, the right arm starts straightening which helps close the clubface. After impact, with the clubshaft pointing to the target, the clubface is now 90 degrees closed to the target. What the myth about Ben Hogan asks us to believe is that as the club head moves on its arc or circular path the club head closes 90 degrees as it travels a distance of a couple of feet, then quits closing for a distance of up to 17" and then closes another 90 degrees in a two foot span all at over 100 miles per hour. The tooth fairy is more believable. Try it yourself in ultra slow motion. Take a club and position it in the down-swing halfway down with the clubface 90 degrees open. As you slowly start to release make the clubface square to the ball or target when it is 7-8" short of the ball. As best you can, try to keep that clubface facing the ball and then the target for 7-8" past the ball. Now continue slowly to the point where the clubshaft points to the target while allowing the clubface to rotate 90 degrees closed to the target. It is virtually impossible to do at 1 mph. At 10 mph nobody can manipulate the clubface that way, let alon' trying to accomplish it at 100 mph. The clubface simply is closing at ' very high rate of speed throughout the release, and the release finis'

45 degrees past the ball.

With the club head traveling at speeds of more than 100 mph and the clubface closing 135 degrees during the release (the club head traveling a distance of 4-5') trying to feel and be square to the target at impact is a fools game. Just 2 degrees off at impact can cause disastrous results with a driver. If the release ended at the ball, it would be much easier to feel square at impact. Unfortunately, we have learned that releasing at the ball causes loss of club head speed (loss of distance) and either fat or topped shots. What a dilemma.

Thankfully there is a better way to approach hitting a ball straight. All we have to do is keep the clubface square to ourselves. Try taking a normal stance and setup with a golf club. Notice where the leading edge of the clubface points to in line with your heels. As you make a perfect turn back and your right arm bends on the backswing the leading edge should always point to the very same spot between the heels. The same thing is true on the forward swing--the leading edge of the clubface points to the same spot at all times. This is true as long as the club head is no higher than the tailbone. Why? Because we are actually keeping the leading edge square to a spot with a specific relationship with the center of the circular arc of the swing. Our spine is the center of that circle and our tailbone is the bottom of our spine. In a proper setup the tailbone will be

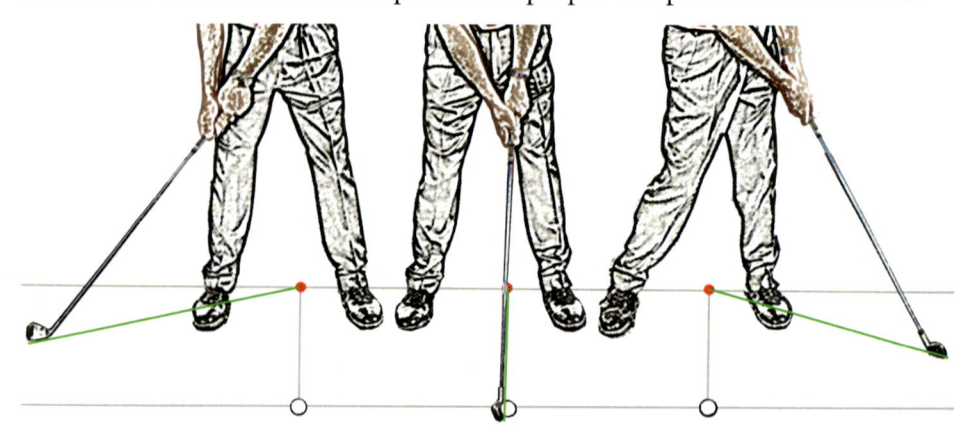

The clubface always stays square to the rotating golfer--not the target.

directly above that line between the heels. With a perfect backswing the clubface always stays perpendicular, or square, to that same spot it originally pointed at. How about when the club head is higher than the tailbone? Then the leading edge will point to that part of the spine that is the same height as the club head. At the top of a full swing the leading edge of the clubface will point to the base of the neck which is the top of the spine.

==The simplicity is that the clubface always stays square to us.== Instead of always trying to open and then close the clubface and get it back to square by impact we can just keep the clubface square at all times--to us. Seems simple in concept, but how easy is it to keep the clubface square to us at all times?

==To keep the clubface square to you at all times, you must keep the hands, arms, shoulders and torso in the same relationship with each other throughout the swing. I call this the Principle of Squareness/Sameness.==
To explain, let me start with some examples of what are not "sameness." At address approximately 2-4" of each arm should be touching the torso in the armpit area. As the club is taken back, if the left arm stays in the same relationship with the torso while the right arm moves away from the body the clubface will be closed. Notice that the leading edge now points to a spot to the right of where it pointed at address. Starting at a perfect address position again, let the left arm swing away from the torso while the right arm stays in the same relationship with the torso. Now the leading edge points to the left of where it did at address and the clubface is open.

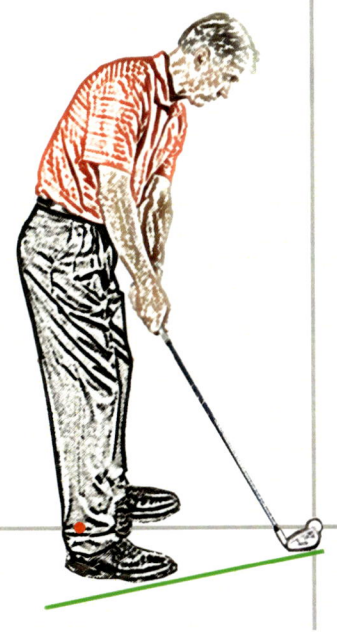

Right upper arm moving away from the torso closes the clubface.

Right upper arm moving closer to the torso opens the clubface.

Lets take a forward swing example. At the finish of the release, the 45, if the right arm is further away from the torso than the left arm the leading edge will be pointing to the right of where it pointed at address and the clubface is now closed. This position, and the resulting hook, are quite common when the release is too early.

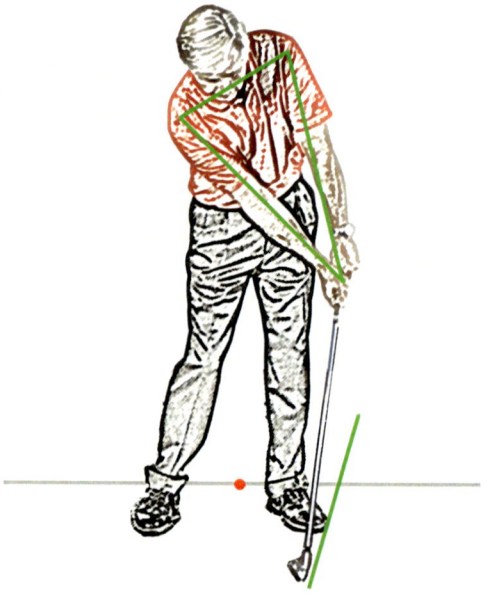

Powering from the arms and shoulders results in the triangle getting ahead of the torso and opening the clubface.

The most common example of not maintaining sameness is this. On the forward swing the player adds power from the left arm/left shoulder area to propel the club forward. This results in the triangle of left arm, shoulders and right arm getting ahead of the torso. The clubface will be open (the leading edge pointing to the left of where it pointed at address) and the ball will be sliced to the right. The more the triangle gets ahead of the torso by impact the larger the slice and the harder it is to "save" the shot by manipulation of the arms and hands. This is the typical slice producing move of a high handicap player.

There are five important parts to keeping the sameness:

1. The shoulders always stay in the same relationship with the torso. Lifting or shrugging either or both shoulders disrupts the swing plane and creates a need for manipulation by the arms, hands and shoulders just to hit the ball. A common mistake is to lift or shrug the left shoulder during the backswing, which causes the golf club to swing on a flatter "layed off" swing plane. Lifting the right shoulder on the backswing causes the golf club to swing on a more upright and "over the top" swing plane. Shrugging or lifting both shoulders during the downswing causes a lifting of the club head which results in thin or topped shots.

2. The elbows always stay the same distance from each other. If they start 6" apart at address they should be 6" apart at the top of the backswing and 6" apart at the end of the follow through.

3. The upper arms stay in the same relationship with the torso. Say that 4" of both right and left triceps are touching your torso in the address position. As your body turns back there should be no change in the amount of each triceps touching the torso. When the body turn stops the arms will continue up as the left arm rotates within the shoulder socket. The left arm maintains the same 4 inches touching of the torso while the right triceps moves away from the torso. The arms continue the sameness by rising an equal amount and at the same rate of speed. As the downswing starts, the turning torso brings the right upper arm back in contact with the right side. Both arms maintain the same amount of touching the torso, 4 inches in this example, until the body stops turning. The arms then continue around the follow through always moving at the same speed and rising away from the torso an equal amount.

4. The one-piece downswing. At the top of the backswing the arms, hands and club are not directly in front of the body as at the address position. Because the right arm has bent approximately 90 degrees the arms and hands have moved considerably further around the swing arc than the torso. Due to wrist bend the club head has moved further yet around the arc. On the downswing the torso, arms, hands and club head should all move at the same rotational speed (equal number of degrees per second) until the release point is reached. At the release point the turning torso has stopped accelerating and the arms, hands and club head start catching up to the torso. At the 45 the arms, hands and club head are all back in front of the torso just as at the address position. If, on the downswing, the club starts moving faster than the arms (wrist power) or the arms start moving faster than the torso (arm power) the sameness cannot be maintained. The result is power and accuracy loss.

5. Wristcock and uncock always need to be on plane. This keeps the hands, wrists and arms in the same relationship with each other throughout the swing.

If sameness is maintained in the hands, arms and torso it is not necessary to roll, maneuver or manipulate the arms and hands to hit the golf ball straight. It actually takes manipulation of the arms and hands to hit anything but a straight shot.

Sameness is remarkably easy to feel. Manipulating one arm or hand more than another is actually much harder than trying to feel and keep the sameness. The feeling is that there is no effort to hit, power, roll, manipulate or anything else with the arms and hands other than to hold on and support the club. Yet the ball will go long and straight. The key to the proper feeling is trying to keep the clubface square to yourself at all times rather than square to the target at impact.

In slow motion practice swings you can check the sameness at the finish of the release (the 45) and where the clubshaft points to the target. Does the leading edge of the clubface point to the right spot? Another good check is to hold your follow through position. Keeping your arms and hands "frozen" turn your body back to an address position. Now lower your arms and hands without changing their relationship with each other. Is the clubface square, open or closed?

Understanding and getting good at applying the Principle of Squareness/ Sameness will probably help most golfers more than any other thing they can do. A significant number of the swing problems of the average golfer are due to manipulations they make to hit the golf ball straight.

Sameness on the backswing.   Sameness at the top.   Sameness at the finish of the release.

CHAPTER 6: THE TURN BLOCKERS

In the previous chapters we have learned how to create efficient power, how to make solid contact with the ball and how to hit a golf ball straight. In theory that should cover everything we need to know to hit good golf shots. In practice it isn't that easy. There are two very common swing errors that cause problems in the turn of the torso. Those errors cause loss of power, unsolid contact and loss of accuracy. I call them the swing blockers.

The first swing blocker is the head. Let me give you an analogy. Imagine a baseball pitcher looking at the third baseman as he released the pitch. He certainly wouldn't have as much velocity as normal and his accuracy would be terrible. The reason is that the head is blocking the turn of the upper body, not allowing the right arm and shoulder area to rotate fully toward the target. Pitchers often turn their heads toward third base on their windup, or backward motion. But they always turn their heads toward the very spot that they are releasing or throwing to prior to the release.

The same thing is true in a golf swing. What we are releasing to is 45 degrees past our straight-ahead address position. If a golfer tightens his neck and upper shoulder muscles to keep his head down, the turn is restricted and the turning body stops accelerating too early. The release automatically starts too early with the result of a scruffy (fat or thin) hit on the ball, a loss of power and a tendency to pull or hook the ball.

So why would anyone tighten their neck and head muscles in order to keep their head down or their "eyes on the ball." Because that is what they were taught to do. That is the single most taught swing advice in the history of the game and it is completely wrong. Not only does it lead to fat and thin shots, loss of power and loss of accuracy, it can cause neck and upper back (shoulder blade area) problems. The high speed twisting of the neck and upper back area in the release combined with tight muscles in that area can and does cause damage and pain for a lot of golfers. Yet what golfer today has not been told at one time or another to "keep your head down" or "keep your eye on the ball". Actually, that last piece of advice, if followed properly, is very good. As soon as the golf ball is struck it is traveling well out in front of the golfer, so to keep your eye on the ball the head needs to turn and not stay down.

In the perfect swing the neck and shoulder area muscles should be relaxed throughout the swing, allowing the head to swivel with the momentum of the swing. So to stop the problem of blocking the turning motion with the head, consciously relax the neck and shoulder area at address and just keep it relaxed throughout the swing.

Anyone who watches tournament golf on TV has seen Annika Sorenstam and David Duval, both former Number 1 ranked players in the world, turn their heads to the left of the ball prior to impact. They both seem to be looking 5 to 20 yards ahead of the ball at impact, depending on the shot. Mechanically this is very sound, way better than keeping your head glued down toward the ball. But since it requires manipulation in order to move the head early, it doesn't qualify as a perfect swing technique. However, it does work as a way out of the "keeping the head down" problem. If you have difficulty keeping your neck and shoulder area relaxed throughout the swing, practice moving the head to look way in front of the ball by impact. Golfers with chronic neck and shoulder blade problems may want to emulate Annika and David on every swing--there is no sense playing in pain.

After hundreds of years of brainwashing by generation after generation of golfers, including some of the best instructors and players in the world, I am sure I haven't convinced everybody that their head doesn't have to stay down and still until well beyond impact. The usual retort I hear is "but if you look up it will pull your body up with it and then you top the ball." Wrong. You would give yourself serious whiplash before any movement of the head would cause your body to be moved by it. The truth is that the head is the only part of the body you CAN move and not cause any movement or change in direction of the golf club. Bend the arms--the club

Moving the head will not cause any movement of the golf club.

moves. Change your torso tilt--the club goes with it. Flex your ankles, sway your hips, cock your wrists--well, you get the idea. Grab a club, take an address position and make all the motions you can with your head. As you can see, the club did not move. Neither did any other body part. Now, from an address position, keep your head still but change the tilt of your spine in any direction you please. Notice the head seems to be moving. In reality, the head is staying in the same relation with the body. The head is staying still, but it is being moved by the body. If that is a tough concept, think about this. If you stand perfectly still are you indeed still or are you traveling approximately 1700 mph? The earth we stand on may be rotating that fast and traveling around the sun as well. But we are considered standing still when we are not moving in relation to the earth.

The bottom line is that there is nothing good accomplished by trying to keep the head down as long as possible, and it does cause poor golf shots and pain.

The second turn blocker is the legs. In the perfect turn the oblique muscles in the back and sides cause the torso to turn. The turning torso causes the shoulders to turn and the hips to turn--unless the legs restrict that turn.

On the backswing, the turning torso causes the right hip to rotate away from the target line, which in turn pulls the right knee back toward the right heel. The right leg therefore straightens somewhat. It doesn't straighten all the way because the hips are only turned 45 degrees away from straight forward. This describes the hip and leg action in a perfect swing, where the turning torso does all the work and the hips and legs merely support and go along for the ride.

Unfortunately, many golfers have been taught to keep their right knee flexed the same on their backswing as at address. Because of the way we are built there are three possible outcomes of this action. First, the backswing torso turn could be severely restricted and the loaded arms do not go back very far on plane. This is wonderful for short shots around the green but won't hit a ball very far.

Second, the backswing torso turn could be severely restricted by the legs but the arms are allowed to swing up above plane for a full swing. This is termed a disconnect of the arms from the body and requires a difficult manipulation of the arms and hands to bring the club back to the ball solidly and accurately.

The third scenario is where the torso keeps turning on the backswing while the right knee stays in the same flexion. This results in the hips shifting toward the target--a reverse weight shift. Once again, considerable manipulation is

Keeping right knee stationary on backswing can cause a reverse weight shift.

needed just to strike the ball solidly and accurately, and there will always be a loss of power.

There is one more motion of the legs that causes an improper turn of the torso on the backswing. If the legs pull the hips laterally away from the target, the common sway, the hips will not be able to rotate properly and the turning torso motion will be restricted.

As with the backswing, the perfect turn on the forward swing starts with a rotation of the torso pulling the left hip away from the target line. This pulls the left knee toward and over the left heel. Since the hips end up turned a full 90 degrees left of their address position the left leg should be virtually straight at the end of the follow through. Approximately 90% of the weight should be supported on the left heel area with only 10% supported by the right toes. But again the legs are frequently the blockers of this perfect turning action.

If the backs of the legs, the hamstring and calve muscles, are too tight or stiff, the turning torso will not be able to pull the left knee over the left heel. It is not unusual to see even accomplished players tighten their calve muscles in the back of their lower legs and actually be on their toes at impact. This usually causes only minor restriction of the torso turn, but it takes quite a bit of athletic talent to hit the ball solidly.

The worst blocking by the legs is by tightening the back of the upper legs, the hamstrings, and/or the buttocks. The resulting restriction on the forward torso turn leads to several major problems. First, the player's hips won't move enough, so the turn forward stops accelerating too early causing an early release. Fat shots, topped shots, bad hooks, even whiffs can result if the legs block the turning motion badly enough. Another scenario when the hips are blocked from moving is that the shoulders turn independently out and around the hips--the over the top swing. Although the club may strike the ball solidly, the club is not on a path to the target. Pulled shots and weak slices are the normal result. Making matters worse, when the club is swung forward with considerable speed and the hips are not allowed to turn enough, there is a high speed twisting of the lower back area. Pain and chiropractors are soon to follow.

After all of the bad news about the legs blocking the turn, here is some good news. Just by relaxing the backs of the legs, the calves and the hamstrings, as well as the buttocks throughout the swing, the perfect turn will pull the legs into the correct positions. If the legs have been a problem in the past, try this practice routine. Start in an address position without a golf club and your hands about 6" apart. As you make a turn back, watch your right knee to see that it straightens slightly and moves toward the right heel. At the end of this practice backswing the arms will be bent somewhat and the hands will still be 6" apart and approximately hip high. You should feel a significant weight shift to the right heel area.

When the backswing motion is easy to do, add the forward swing. Now shift your eyes to your left knee as you smoothly and slowly turn forward to the target. Watch the left knee straighten and move over the left heel. At the finish of this forward practice swing the arms will be in front of you with the hands still 6" apart and about hip high. Approximately 90 % of your weight should be on the left heel area.

If the practice routine is hard to do, it may feel like you have to use your legs to create the proper motion. With practice, the legs will learn how to relax and go along for the ride. The perfect swing requires the turning of the torso to cause the movement of the hips and legs, which is much simpler, efficient, powerful and accurate.

Once the practice without a club becomes easy, add a golf club but still no ball. Keep your turn speeds low at first and see if your turn can make your hips and legs move properly. Check your balance and weight distribution at the top of the backswing and again at the top of the follow through. When you can turn at full speed and the balance is perfect back and through you are ready for golf balls.

The perfect turning motion comes from our torso--our center. The blockers are above and below our center. ==The key to not blocking the turning motion is relaxation in both the neck/shoulder top area and the back of the legs/buttocks area.==

Perfect follow through when legs and head do not block the turn.

CHAPTER 7: SUPPORT FOR THE SWING

In the previous chapters the perfect swinging motion has been presented. That motion requires a great deal of movement by the turning torso and the swinging arms. Clubhead speeds may reach speeds well in excess of 100 mph. All of that motion at high speed causes forces that must be dealt with or the structure of the swing will collapse. If those forces are not held in check the posture and balance of the body will be lost and the club will fly away on the wrong path. The results are not pretty--miss-hits, mis-direction or even whiffs.

The swinging motion needs to be supported by many of the muscles and bones of the body. Just standing takes a certain amount of muscular effort in the legs, hips, back and neck area. If you have ever had to stand straight for a length of time you know how certain muscles get tired just support-ing you. It takes even more muscular effort, especially in the back area, to support you in the proper bent forward golf posture. When you swing a golf club some muscles are active--the obliques and lats in the back--to create the incredible power of the golf swing. The rest of the muscles in the body are passive as far as power goes, but many have a very important job in supporting the perfect swinging motion.

Let's start at the lowest pillar of support, the feet and ankles, and go up-ward. At address, the weight of the body is centered in the arches of the foot. If you look at your feet, you will notice that the arches are not cen-tered in the foot. It is farther from the center of the arch to the toes than it is to the heel. So in effect, the proper balance point is slightly toward our heels. On the backswing, the perfect turn pulls the right knee back toward the right heel, which moves the weight towards the right heel. The weight does not move all the way to the heel, which would pull the right toes off the ground slightly, but only halfway from the arch to the heel. On the forward swing the turning motion pulls the left knee back and over the left heel, and the weight goes with it. The left toes will be pulled very slightly off the ground at the end of the follow through and 90% of the body weight will be supported by the left heel area. The other 10% of the weight will be supported by the right toes.

It is important to have very flexible, relaxed ankles when swinging a golf club. The turning torso should pull the hips, which in turn pulls the knees, which pulls on the ankles. On the backswing the right ankle should straighten some as the left ankle bends more. On the forward swing the left ankle straightens with the turning motion and the right ankle first bends and then straightens for the follow through. All of this action in the ankles should not be created by using the muscles in the leg and ankle area, however. Relaxing the ankle area allows the proper motion. If the ankles are too stiff the proper motion and weight transfer of the golf swing suffers. The proper body turn will be restricted, causing necessary manipulations and loss of power and accuracy.

Next up the support chain is the hips and legs area. The calves, the muscles in the lower leg, need to be relaxed throughout the swing. The same amount of effort used for standing is just perfect for swinging a club. If the calf muscles tighten the ankle joints straighten, which puts the body weight on the toes. You may have seen a few really good tour players, Natalie Gulbis and Laura Davies come to mind, who come up on their toes through the impact area. It takes a very talented athlete to make such a move and become so accomplished at the game. Just the balance factor at such a high swing speed is amazing. Even more difficult is coordinating the compensation move for the lifting up on to the toes. On shorter, slower speed swings these players do not lift up nearly as much as they do on full, high speed swings. As the amount of lift changes, so must the amount of compensation for that lift. Hard work and talent can sometimes make up for a swing error. Sometimes.

Whether we are just standing or we are swinging a golf club, we need both our hamstrings and our quadriceps, the muscles of the upper leg. The hamstring muscles, the back side of the upper leg, are the benders of the leg. If they tighten too much a golfers' legs will bend or buckle on the downswing. They also can be very restrictive of the turning motion, so

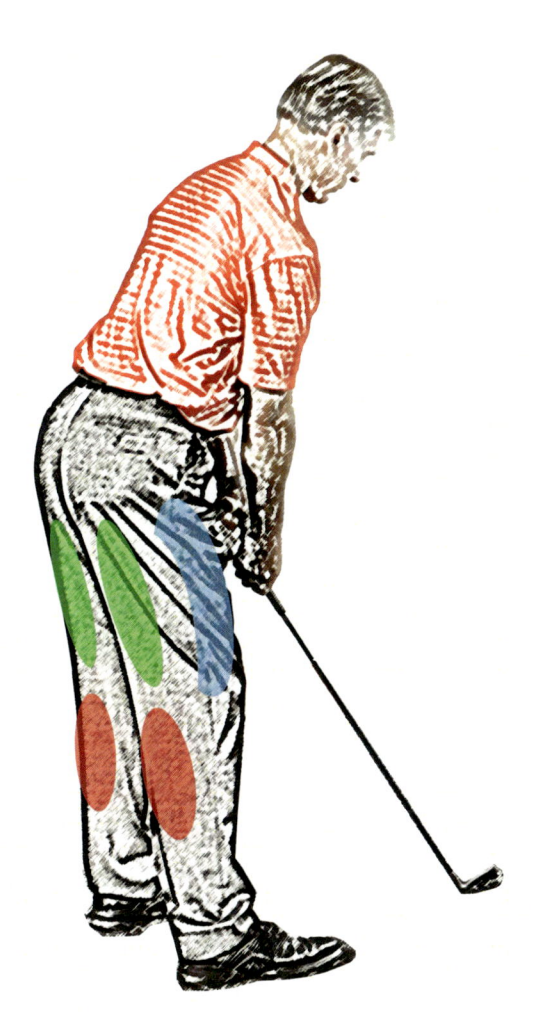

Hamstrings - Green, Calves - Red, Quads - Blue.

The quadriceps muscles, the top side of the upper leg, are the extenders of the leg. By staying strong , the quads will allow a natural straightening of the right leg on the backswing and a natural straightening of the left leg on the forward swing. It is important to keep the quads strong so there is no collapsing of the legs on the downswing. The faster the downswing club head speed, the more downward force is created, which means more support in the quads is necessary. So the quads are very important muscles in supporting the golf swing.

Just above the hips are the muscles of the torso. The abdominal muscles, in the stomach area, bend the torso forward. Although golfers need to bend forward in the proper golf posture, the abs do nothing to hold us in that posture. A common misuse of the abs is to tighten them during the downswing, causing a drop in the upper body and a resulting fat shot. The oblique muscles, responsible for powering the golf swing, add structural support for the turning torso as well.

==The lower and middle back muscles on each side of the spine, commonly called the extensor and erector muscle groups, are very important. They are most responsible for holding our posture while we turn our torso.== There are very few things people do in their lives that require as much muscular effort from their extensor and erector muscle groups. For that reason, most golfers are relatively weak in those muscles. The best players in the world take thousands of swings each week, so their back muscles are very strong. For them the support by the back muscles seems easy. The occasional golfer and the several times a week golfer who never practices are usually compromised by an inability to hold their posture while swinging, especially late on the back nine.

Extender and Extensor muscle groups.

The lats, in the middle and upper back area, not only lift the arms during the backswing, but they keep the arms from flying away from the body due to the centrifugal force created by the turning torso. ==The more club head speed created by the turn, the more tension or tightness needed in the lats to keep the arms in the same relationship with the torso.==

The final support area is the arms and hands. ==The biceps are the benders of the arm and are not necessary for any support (or power) in the golf swing.== Although the right arm does bend in the backswing, the right bicep should have nothing to do with it. If it did, it would require an intentional letting go of the right bicep tension at precisely the right time for the release. At the ever increasing speed of the downswing that would be incredibly difficult.

It is the triceps, the under side of the upper arm, that are the main structural support for the swing. The triceps job is to straighten the arms. Yet the left triceps are in a very weak position next to the chest at the top of the backswing. So the left arm cannot keep itself straight in a perfect swing. It is the right triceps that keeps the left arm straight just by keeping steady pressure throughout the swing. Since the right arm cannot pull the left arm out of its socket, if a golfer adheres to a perfect swing plane and the principle of squareness/sameness as explained in earlier chapters, the right arm will bend despite the strong right triceps. And the left arm will be straight--a structurally perfect position--at the top of the backswing.

Since it is hard to keep the right triceps strong and the left triceps soft, I recommend keeping equal pressure in both. Mechanically the left triceps doesn't add anything but simple is always better. How strong or firm should the triceps muscles be? The longer the backswing the stronger the support that is needed to keep the left arm straight. That said, if the biceps muscles in both arms are relaxed, it doesn't take that much effort in the triceps. I have seen students who habitually had a left arm breakdown learn to support with the triceps, relax the biceps and begin keeping their left arm straight in just a few minutes.

One final note about the triceps. Too much pressure or tightness in the triceps will keep the arms straight well past the finish of the release at the 45 and can cause damage to the tendons and ligaments in the arms. The arms need to naturally bend at the elbow as the club completes its arc to the follow through. So, enough pressure is needed to keep the left arm straight on the backswing, but not enough to keep it straight beyond the club pointing at the target.

Finally we have the forearms, wrists and hands area. In the perfect swing they are not used to power the club in any direction because of the loss of power and accuracy that would result. So they are entirely being used for support of the swing. We will cover the grip in the next chapter, but there are two important considerations regarding how the hands and wrists support the golf swing. The first consideration is the position of the hands on the golf club. At the top of the backswing the left hand, except for the thumb, is on top of the grip. This is a weak supporting position. The right arm and hand are under the grip and under the left thumb, which is a strong supporting position. Also, at impact the left hand is in front of the grip and clubshaft while the right palm and index finger are behind the shaft. So the left hand can offer little support for the swinging club when it meets resistance in the striking of the ball and ground. The right hand is in perfect position to support the left thumb, left hand and the golf club throughout the swing.

Secondly, the swing builds up centrifugal force on the downswing, which tries to throw the club away from the center of our turning body. Pressure on the top side of the grip by the thumbs would cause an early throwout of the club, an unwanted early release. But pressure with the fingers on the underneath side of the grip add the proper support to resist the club being released early by centrifugal force.

The proper pressure in the forearms and fingers should be strong enough to resist the throwaway of the club by centrifugal force but not so much that it restricts the wrist cocking and uncocking motion. Pressure of 5 or 6 on a 1-10 scale is appropriate for full speed swings. It is most important to keep the forearm, wrist, hand and finger pressures feeling the same throughout the swing. Change in those pressures can cause the club to move off plane or change the clubface angles. Once again, sameness is the answer for perfect shots.

CHAPTER 8: THE PERFECT GRIP

The perfect swinging motion will not result in a perfect shot unless the grip is perfect as well. Although the hands have no job in the swing other than to hold on and support, the alignment of the grip is of utmost importance. ==To hit a ball straight without any manipulation with the hands and arms, it is necessary to have a square grip.==

There are two fundamental requirements in making the perfect grip. ==First, the grip needs to be taken with the leading edge of the clubface square to the player (as explained in the Principle of squareness/sameness) with the clubshaft pointed at the left shoulder.== Taking the grip with the clubshaft pointing at the belly button results in an open clubface at impact. This is because in a perfect impact position the clubshaft is always pointing to the left shoulder.

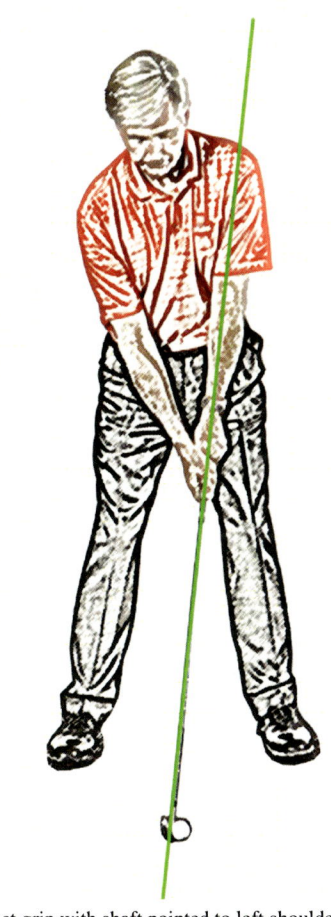

Perfect grip with shaft pointed to left shoulder and clubface square to target line.

==Secondly, the position of the hands on the grip is always dependent upon the placement of the ball in the stance.== Think of it this way. For a driver, we need to play the ball at or near the low point of the perfect swing, which is directly across from the left shoulder. Say we took a perfectly square grip for a driver setup and then, without changing our grip, moved the club 6" back in the stance as for a wedge shot. The clubface would be considerably open to the target line at the ball. Hitting a ball with such a setup would result in a slice unless major manipulation was used to

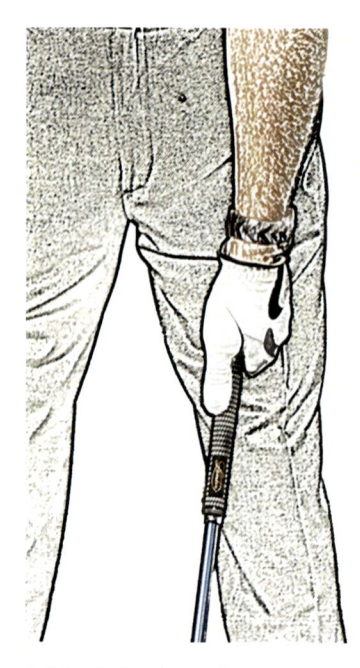

Left hand placed properly on grip.

square up the clubface. As explained before, the swing moves the club in an arc, or part of a circle. As we move the club head further to the right (back in the stance) the clubface points further to the right of the target. So to hit a ball straight without manipulation we have to change our grip alignments to allow our clubface to be square at address and impact for each new ball position.

To place the left hand properly on the club we first approximate where the ball will be in our stance, and put the club head on the ground square to an intended target. With the clubshaft pointed at the left shoulder, place the heel pad (pad at the base of the hand on the little finger side, between the palm and back of the hand) on the top of the grip. Obviously, if the ball position changes, the top of the grip will change as well. Next, place the left index finger middle knuckle directly under the grip. Allow the fingers to wrap around and hold the club while the thumb is placed slightly to the right of the top of the grip. It is important to place the thumb far enough down the grip past the index finger to allow the grip pressure to be under the grip, in the fingers. A short thumb position puts grip pressure on top of the grip, which encourages an early release on the downswing. When the left heel pad and index finger are positioned on the top and bottom of the grip, the proper wristcock causes the clubshaft to stay in line with the left arm. The back of the left wrist will be parallel to the clubshaft.

The left heel pad and knuckle can be rotated somewhat clockwise on the grip and still approximate a perfect grip. By maintaining the same relationship with the left hand and clubshaft, the wristcock can still keep the clubshaft in line with the left arm. The left wrist will then be in a bent position at the top of the swing. The problem is in keeping the bent wrist

The slightly rotated left hand grip shown in the picture on the left can approximate the square left hand grip pictured on the right by maintaining a slightly cupped position throughout the swing.

position through impact. If centrifugal force causes the wrist to straighten, the clubface will close and a hooked shot results. With pressure in the left wrist area to counter centrifugal force, the sameness can be maintained. While not a perfect grip, since extra pressure is needed in the left hand, it approximates a perfect grip.

If the left heel pad and index finger middle knuckle are rotated counter clockwise on the grip (a so called weak grip) perfect shots are very difficult to hit.. Weak, crooked shots--mostly to the right-- are the usual result and there is potential to damage the tendons and ligaments in the left hand and wrist.

Whereas the back of the left hand has a relationship with the clubshaft, the right hand has a relationship with the clubface. The right palm should face the same direction as the clubface for all straight shots. The right palm makes a tongue-and-groove fit with the left thumb and should face the target. The last knuckle of the right index finger should be placed directly under the grip. Finally, the right thumb should be placed to the left of the

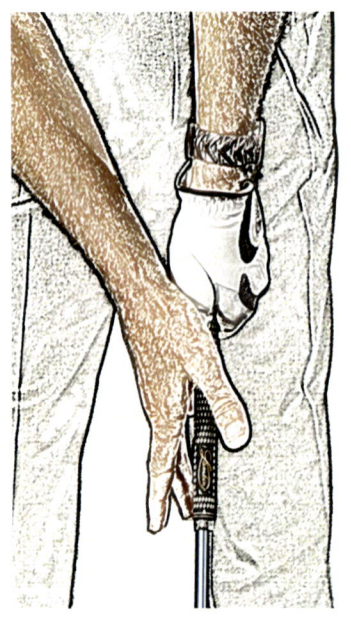

Putting the right palm properly on the left thumb.

top of the grip. Allow the fingers to grip the club.

With the right hand placed correctly, notice what we have done. First, the palm of the right hand is a guide for the clubface, as is the inside edge of the right index finger which is touching the grip. Just as importantly, the palm and index finger are on plane and behind the shaft--they are the main pressure points in the hands that transfer the force of the swinging motion to the club and allow for thrusting through the resistance of hitting the ball and ground. If they are not positioned properly there will be power and accuracy loss.

You will also notice that the right index finger is separated somewhat from the rest of the fingers. This is a correct position. Imagine throwing a baseball. You had two fingers behind the ball for support and guidance and the throwing motion power was transferred through those two fingers to the ball. If the fingers were directly behind the ball and stayed there throughout, a straight fastball was the result. If the fingers were placed to the side or allowed to rotate to the side during the delivery the result was a curving of the ball flight. It is exactly the same in golf. If the inside of the right index finger and the palm are positioned directly behind the grip and allowed to remain square to the center of the arc of the swing, the ball will fly straight.

As for the right thumb, why do we put it off to the left side of the grip? If the thumb were on the top

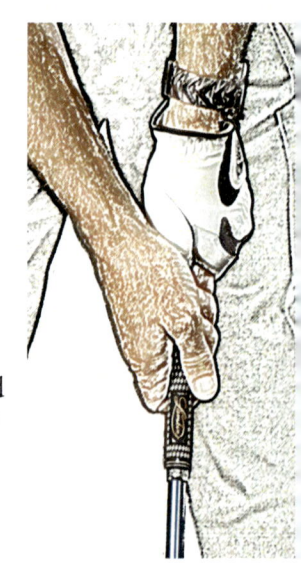

Close-up of perfect grip.

of the grip, the only motion it could make would cause either an early release of the wristcock or an off plane movement in the hitting area. Since the thumb can cause problems and cannot help in any way, it is important to place the thumb off to the side where it cannot cause any bad shots.

Finally, let's take another look at the back of the left wrist. When setting up for a driver shot the clubshaft should look straight up and down when viewed from facing the golfer. The back of the left wrist should be flat and facing the target. A line drawn down the back of the left wrist would go straight down to the ground, perfectly vertical. As the ball position moves back in the stance, the back of the left wrist will face more to the right of the target, but will always stay parallel to the clubshaft. This is because the positioning of the left heel pad and middle knuckle of the index finger is moved to stay on the top and bottom sides of the grip. Since the grip changes as the ball position changes , a line drawn down the back of the left hand will still be perfectly vertical.

I must be forgetting something, you're saying. Should you use an overlap grip, an interlocking grip, a ten-finger grip? Actually, any of the above are just fine for a perfect grip. Perfect alignments are what is necessary for the perfect grip. How the hands interlock or not doesn't preclude the ability to hit straight and long shots. Let's see how the different grips stack up against each other.

The interlocking grip works just fine for hitting a golf ball solid and straight without manipulation, but there is some loss of support in the right hand and wrist area. A player with strong wrists and hands should have no trouble with the proper support, though weaker players may need to use a different grip. The biggest concern with an interlocking grip is the tendency to create an arthritic condition in the little finger of the right hand. Many years of hitting golf balls with the little finger spread away from the next finger and hooked around the left index finger has been the cause of much pain for older golfers.

The right little finger overlapping the left index finger is also fine for hit-

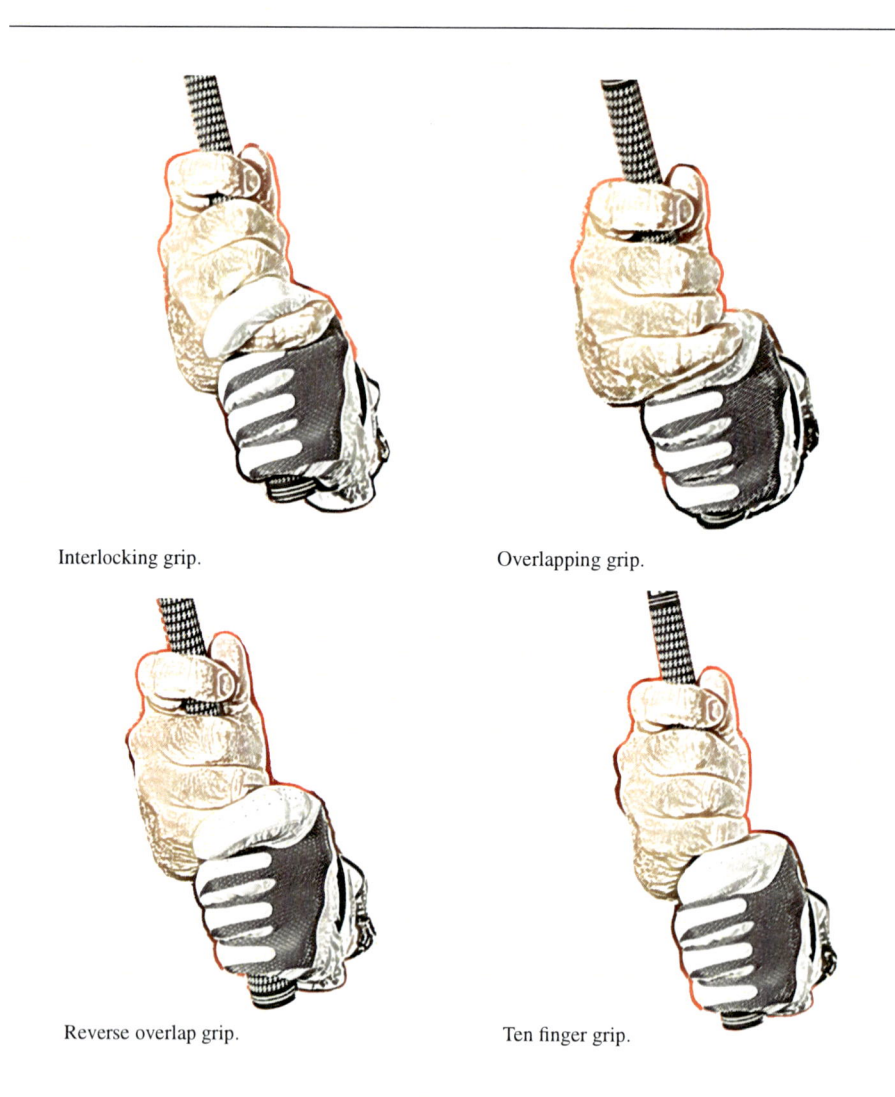

Interlocking grip.

Overlapping grip.

Reverse overlap grip.

Ten finger grip.

ting shots and there is no tendency to cause arthritis. The drawback is an even greater loss of support of the club by the right hand and wrist.

The left index finger overlapping the right little finger is again fine for hitting perfect shots and there is excellent support for the club by the right hand and wrist. This would be my favorite grip, except that the tip of the little finger on the right hand tends to get pinched between the grip and the base of the left index finger. For someone playing and practicing a lot this grip could cause the little finger to get sore and painful.

The 10 finger grip, where there is no overlapping or interlocking of the fingers is once again good for hitting perfect shots. It also allows for great support for the club by the right hand and wrist. One knock on the so-called baseball grip is that the hands are not as close together as with over-lapping or interlocking grips and don't work quite as well as a unit. But because the hands don't do anything except hold on and support the club, I don't buy that argument. I switched to the 10 finger grip over 15 years ago and have found only one minor drawback. The end of the right hand little finger gets rubbed by the upper part of the left index finger. I wrap that little finger with gauze-tape so that I don't get a sore callous or blister. You can also spread the hands apart just enough to avoid the rubbing.

Checking where the v's formed between the thumb and index fingers are pointing, or how many knuckles you can see at address may seem like simple grip guides. The problem is that those guides are very inaccurate and have nothing to do with the proper alignment of the hands on the grip. Since simplicity is important let me give you this six part method of put-ting on the proper grip. The grip should be put on in this exact order.
1) Put the left heel pad on top of the grip.
2) Put the middle joint of the left index finger directly under the grip.
3) Put the left thumb slightly right of the top of the grip.
4) Put the right palm in a tongue-and-groove fit with the left thumb and facing the target.
5) Put the last joint of the right index finger directly under the grip.
6) Put the right thumb on the left side of the grip.

An even simpler version would be: Left--heel pad, index finger, thumb. Right--palm, index finger, thumb.

The last thing you should know about the grip is how much pressure to apply. There has always been debate about how hard or light to hold the club. My advice is to be somewhere in the 5-6 range on a 1-10 scale. More pressure can cause a restriction of the wrist cock and uncocking motion. Less pressure can cause a feeling of losing the club, and a tightening of the pressure on the downswing is likely. Keeping the same pressure in the hands throughout the swing is imperative in making the perfect swinging motion. That pressure should always be in the fingers and right palm areas and not in the top of the hands area.

CHAPTER 9: PERFECT SETUP

Power and accuracy in a perfect golf swing come from a perfect turning motion propelling the arms, hands and club in the proper manner. But improper posture or alignments can cause many problems in creating the perfect golf shots. Lets start with perfect posture.

The turn of the torso is around our spine. The spine makes a natural s-curve, but ideally when we stand tall (perfect military posture) a straight and vertical line would touch our buttocks, the middle of our back for several inches, and the back of our head. The closer we can come to that perfect posture when bent forward addressing a golf ball the better. Most golfers have too much bowing in the middle of the back and virtually all golfers have too much bowing in the neck/head area. Any bowing or dipping forward by the spine from the ideal natural straight line causes extra difficulty in creating the perfect turn. As the lower part of the spine turns perfectly the bowed upper spine is forced to move laterally back on the backswing and forward on the forward swing. This results in the upper torso and head moving sideways in the swing. The lower the back of the head is from a straight line drawn from the buttocks along the edge of the back the more the head and upper torso will move laterally in a perfect turn. Although mechanically sound, there are several problems with this type

Perfect posture at address.

of turn.

First, our oblique muscles that we use to turn our torso around our spine work more precisely if they are not bent in the middle. Second, the lateral movement of the head causes the eyes to move as well. While a little head movement is not a problem, a movement of six inches back on the backswing can be very disturbing to a golfer trying to make clean contact with the ball. The biggest problem is that golfers, trying to reduce the lateral movement of the head, turn around the middle of their body instead of their spine and create a reverse weight shift.

The closer the back of the head is to a straight line drawn from the buttocks past the edge of the back the less the head will move in a perfect turn around the spine. If the back of the head is in perfect alignment and the head does not swivel during the backswing, the head could stay perfectly still during the backswing--in theory. However, there are very few golfers who achieve this perfect posture. The good news is that when the back of the head is only a couple of inches lower than what would be perfect posture the 2-3" of head movement created by a perfect turn causes no real problem.

To get as close as possible to perfect posture in the spinal area take a look at the buttocks when you are at address. It should not look like a dog with his tail between his legs, nor like a duck tail which would create more curve than necessary in the lower spine. Right in the middle is perfect. Next, look at the head and neck area. The back of the neck should be pulled back as far as possible. This should not raise the chin out of an ordinary relationship with the neck. If this is difficult to do, talk to a doctor or physical therapist to find out how to improve your posture.

We now know that the spine should be as straight as possible when viewed from behind the player on the target line. How about when viewed face on? Many instructors teach a tilt of the spine to the right. This creates two problems. First, the turn is much more difficult when the spine is tilted sideways versus being vertical. If you aren't sure you agree with this statement try a little test. Stand straight up and then turn your torso in both directions. Pretty easy to stay in the straight up posture. Now, standing straight again, tilt your body to the right and try turning the torso again. Much more difficult to keep the same posture as well as turn with any speed. ==Second, tilting to the right causes the club to bottom out further back in the stance--not a good idea for most golfers since their clubs already bottom out too far back.==

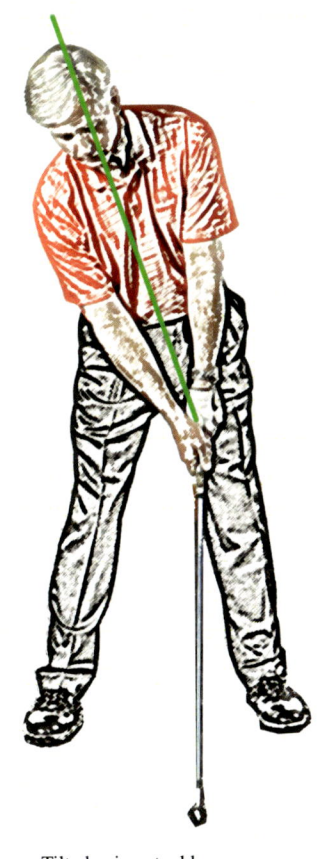

Tilted spine at address.

Let's continue with the proper setup with other parts of the body. ==The knees should be only slightly bent.== The more bend in the knees, the more they restrict the proper turn. Balance while swinging is also compromised when knee bend is excessive. The old adage of getting into an athletic position is great when playing defense in basketball but doesn't apply to golf. The basketball player needs to be ready to move forward, backward and sideways. The golfer does not. He needs to have a pivot or turning motion. If the basketball player needs to pivot he drops a foot backward. The golfer would be in serious trouble if he tried dropping a foot back during his swing.

The weight should be centered equally on the arches of the feet at address. Notice that the center of the arch of a foot is somewhat closer to the heel than the toe. As the backswing reaches the top of a full swing, the weight will be distributed approximately 60% right heel area and 40% left inside forefront area. At the end of the follow through the weight will be distributed approximately 90% on the outer left heel area and 10% on the right toe area.

The right foot should be flared slightly to the right of straight forward to ease the backswing turning motion--no more than 10 degrees. Since there is more twisting of the left ankle and knee in the forward swing the foot may be flared out to the left 10-25 degrees. If pain or stiffness in either the left ankle or knee is a problem, open the foot as much as is necessary to reduce pain and improve balance. It is important to keep the legs and feet relaxed throughout the swing to allow the perfect turning motion. Balance, accuracy and power all suffer when the ankle, knee and hip joints are not free to move.

The arms should hang as long as possible (I call it relaxed straight), with 2-5" of the upper arm touching the torso, depending on length of club and size of the chest area. Those golfers with large chests may need longer clubs with flatter lie angles and tilt more from the waist to allow their left arm and torso to keep the same relationship throughout the swing. If the left arm has to swing around a large chest the left arm either becomes higher than the right arm, an open position, or both arms swing too far out from the torso, a too upright position.

When viewing a golfer face on, the clubshaft should always point at the left shoulder at address. This is for every shot and every ball position. If the clubshaft points to the middle of the body at address and we properly hit the ball with the clubshaft pointed at the left shoulder a slight raising of the body or other manipulation during the swing would be necessary to hit the ball solidly. A second manipulation would be necessary to keep from slicing. Once again, you can make this game as difficult as you wish, but the perfect swing requires no manipulations to hit a ball long and straight.

When getting aligned for the perfect swing we need to set our clubface first and then set our body in relation to the clubface and target line. If you remember the principle of squareness/sameness, the leading edge of the clubface always points to a particular spot in the stance when addressing the ball. We found that spot by drawing a line from the ball perpendicular to the target line, to wherever that line crossed a second line across our heels. If the club head was directly over the center of the ball the leading edge would point to that spot. At address the club is slightly behind the ball but still pointing to that same spot. This means that the clubface will be ever so slightly open to the target line at address when hitting the perfectly straight shot.

Any time the golf ball is positioned either in the middle of the stance or forward of center stance the shoulders and torso should be set square to the target line. Since it is almost impossible to see both shoulders at the same time when addressing a golf ball, I suggest using the chest as a guide. If your chest is square to the target line the shoulders will be square as well.

If you position the ball back of the center of the stance the path of the club head in the impact area becomes so inside out that pushes or hooks would result. Adjusting the shoulders and chest to be aligned to the left of the target can bring the inside out delivery right down the target line. Obviously the grip also needs to be changed any time the ball position changes as noted in the previous chapter.

There is leeway in the perfect swing in setting the feet to the target line. We are not kicking the ball, or moving the club with our feet or legs. That said, if the feet get too far out of alignment with the torso it can cause restriction of the turning motion. One generalization--the further forward the ball is positioned ahead of center in the stance the more a slightly closed stance helps in aligning the shoulders and torso square to the target line. The idea is to align the upper body perfectly. Wherever the feet are aligned is just fine if it feels relaxed and doesn't restrict the perfect turning motion in either direction.

The width of the stance depends on the momentum generated by the swing. The momentum of the forward swing should carry the golfer's weight over to the left leg and foot without any pushing from the right leg and foot. If the weight ends up perfectly balanced on the left heel area the stance is most likely the right width. If the momentum of a perfect swing tries to move the weight to the left side but the weight falls back to the right foot, the stance is too wide. If that momentum carries the weight past the left leg so that a step with the right leg is necessary to catch one's balance, the stance is too narrow. For most golfers a shoulder width stance is just right for most full swings. With a driver, which develops more club head speed, the stance may be a couple of inches wider.

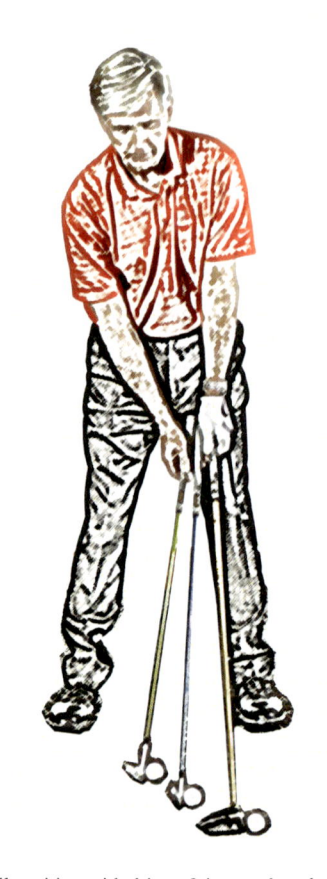

The position of the ball at address is dependent upon the particular shot. For a driver, we want to strike the ball on a level or slightly upward swing path. Since the low point of a perfect swing would be slightly back of opposite the left

Ball position with driver, 3-iron and wedge.

shoulder we should play the golf ball directly opposite that shoulder. The best guide for where the ball is positioned in the stance is the center of the stance. The width of the stance may change from one shot to the next, but the center of the stance is always the center. Since your left shoulder will be 5-7" from your chin, which is in the center of your body, the ball should be played that same 5-7" to the left of opposite your chin for a driver. Both the nose and the chin are excellent guides for ball position because they are centered in the stance and the eyes are located right next to them. Visually it is easy to tell where your chin and nose are in relation to different spots on the ground.

When hitting a golf ball off the ground we need to hit the ball on the downswing. I recommend playing fairway woods and hybrids approximately 3" ahead of the center of the stance for a normal lie and normal trajectory shot. At that point in the stance the club head path will be just slightly on the downswing. Releasing perfectly to the 45 the club head should strike the ball and the ground at the same time. Hybrids, with their large bottoms, may be played in the same location for high trajectory shots or played 2" ahead of center stance for normal trajectory shots. Long irons should be played approximately 2" ahead of center and medium irons only 1" ahead of center stance. Wedges and nine irons are best played right in the center of the stance. At that point in the stance the club head will strike the ball first and then contact the ground under the front edge of the ball with a perfect release. All of the clubs may be moved slightly forward from my recommendations for higher flying shots if the lie of the ball will allow it. For lower ball flights or less than perfect lies the ball may be moved back in the stance several inches. Remember that as the ball is moved forward or backward in the stance the grip must always be adjusted to be square at that point and the body alignment must be adjusted for changes to the club head path in the impact area.

CHAPTER 10: THE PERFECT SWING FUNDAMENTALS

Well, there you have it. The previous chapters of this book give a detailed explanation of the fundamentals of the Perfect Swing Model. Starting with a perfect setup and grip, the swing is powered back and through with a perfect turn around the spine. The club is always swung on plane and the clubface is always square to the center of the arc on which it swings. The release is always to the 45. The obliques and lats actively create power and the rest of the body either just supports or goes along for the ride.

The perfect swing should not seem too complicated or hard to achieve. Any swing could be deemed complicated, but the perfect swing model uses the fewest active muscles and requires no manipulations to hit a golf ball long and straight. The most difficult aspect of learning the perfect swing and applying it is eliminating all the extra motions and effort that robs most golfers of power and accuracy.

Not only is the physical process of the perfect swing easier but the thought process is much less complicated. No longer do golfers need to think about keeping their head down or still, keeping their left arm straight, timing the shoulder turn with their hip turn, staying behind the ball, swinging inside out, pronation and supination of hands and forearms, locking or bracing the right knee, pulling down with the left side, hitting down on the ball, pushing off the right side, or making an early wristcock. These are just a short list of all the bad swing thoughts golfers commonly use that can now be eliminated.

The simplicity of the perfect swing is that once the extraneous muscle effort is gone the mind only needs to concern itself with the active muscles used for the swing. Thinking about the perfect turn back and through with the obliques in the back and rib area is the ultimate simple thought. Certain muscle groups, such as the triceps in the arms and the extensor and extender groups in the back, need to learn how to provide the proper support, but with practice they get so good at it that no thought of them is necessary. So the simple thought process is more of a feel thought--turn and load, turn and release. Feel the load and release of pressure where the arms connect with the torso. For those with good visualizing skills, it can really simplify things to visualize yourself turning your torso perfectly and loading and releasing the arms perfectly. Looking at your body turn in a mirror as you make practice swings can be invaluable--when the swing looks perfect in the mirror pay attention to what it feels like.

There are a lot of different ways to swing a golf club. Some are just a lot harder to do well than others. Trying to do things that go against the human body's natural motions or violate the laws of physics and geometry leads to poor results and frustration. The perfect swing model requires the least amount of muscular effort to create powerful and accurate golf shots. It does not violate any laws of physics, geometry or fight our body's natural motions. The perfect swing is attainable by most golfers. Just understanding it and applying some of the fundamentals can help everybody who plays the game.

The Fundamentals of the Perfect Swing Model

1) Square grip and body alignments.

2) Perfect posture and balance at address and throughout the swing.

3) Power is created by turning the torso with the obliques and an automatic loading and releasing of the arms and wrists.

4) The club is always swung on plane.

5) The Principle of 45 degrees.

6) The Principle of Squareness/Sameness.

ABOUT THE AUTHOR

Fred Haney began playing golf with his father in 1958 at the age of 10. Winning the Oregon State High School Golf Championship Tournament brought Fred the opportunity to play golf in college for the University of Oregon. He was captain of the team his junior and senior years and won the Pac-8 Northern Division Tournament his senior year.

In 1971 Fred won the United States Public Links Championship at Papago Golf Course in Phoenix, Arizona. A medal play event at that time, this win has been the highlight of his playing career.

Fred has won over 80 tournaments in his lifetime as either an amateur or professional golfer. Major wins include the Washington Open, Pacific Northwest PGA, Oregon PGA, Oregon Senior Open, Washington Senior Open and Pacific Northwest Senior PGA.

As an instructor, Fred has had many accomplished students. Two boys have earned Oregon High School First Team All-State Golf Team honors. One of those, Jeremy Parrott went on to earn NCAA First Team All-American Golf Team honors while at The University of Georgia. Another student won the Oregon Girls State High School Golf Tournament. Two other students have won the Northwest Open and another student won the Oregon PGA Championship. One Oregon Amateur Championship final match pitted two of Fred's students against each other.

Fred currently is a Teaching Professional at The Reserve Vineyards and Golf Club in Aloha, Oregon.

NOTES: